BRIGHT
IDEA
BOOKS

MARLEY
Dias

by Jenny Benjamin

CAPSTONE PRESS
a capstone imprint

Bright Idea Books are published by Capstone Press
1710 Roe Crest Drive, North Mankato, Minnesota 56003
www.mycapstone.com

Library of Congress Cataloging-in-Publication Data
Names: Benjamin, Jenny, author.
Title: Marley Dias / by Jenny Benjamin.
Description: North Mankato, Minnesota : Capstone Press, [2019] | Series:
  Bright idea books | Series: Influential people | Includes bibliographical
  references and index. | Audience: Grades 4-6. | Audience: Ages 9-12.
Identifiers: LCCN 2018036587 | ISBN 9781543557916 (hardcover : alk. paper) |
  ISBN 9781543558234 (ebook) | ISBN 9781543560367 (paperback)
Subjects: LCSH: Dias, Marley (Marley Emerson)--Juvenile literature. | African
  American girls--United States--Biography--Juvenile literature. | Community
  activists--United States--Biography--Juvenile literature. | Young
  volunteers in social service--United States--Biography--Juvenile
  literature. | Jamaican Americans--Biography--Juvenile literature. |
  Children of immigrants--United States--Biography--Juvenile literature. |
  Social action--United States--Juvenile literature.
Classification: LCC E185.97.D53 B45 2019 | DDC 361.20973--dc23
LC record available at https://lccn.loc.gov/2018036587

Editorial Credits
Editor: Claire Vanden Branden
Designer: Becky Daum
Production Specialist: Colleen McLaren

Photo Credits
AP Images: Jordan Strauss/Invision, cover; Getty Images: Dia Dipasupil/Getty Images
Entertainment, 24–25, Gustavo Caballero/Getty Images Entertainment, 21; iStockphoto: atm2003,
10–11; Newscom: Cheriss May/NurPhoto/Sipa USA, 17, Robin Platzer/Twin Images/Avalon.
red, 26; Rex Features: Broadimage, 23, JimSmeal, 13, MediaPunch, 18, Michael Buckner/Variety,
14; Shutterstock Images: Danita Delmont, 6–7, Jamie Lamor Thompson, 5, 28, Sean Pavone, 9,
wavebreakmedia, 31

TABLE OF CONTENTS

CHAPTER 1

A
Movement

Marley Dias loves to write and read. One of her favorite books is *Brown Girl Dreaming*. It is written by Jacqueline Woodson. The main **character** is a black girl. She grows up in the 1960s and '70s.

Dias was **inspired** by the books she read. So she started a book drive in 2015. She wanted to collect 1,000 books. The books would have black girls as main characters. The books would go to children in Jamaica.

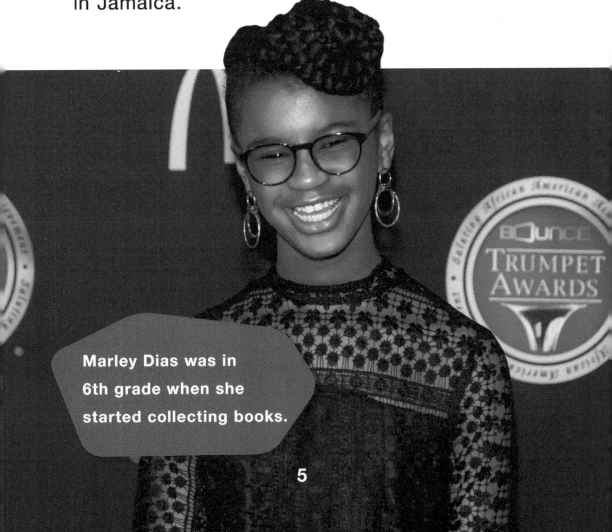

Marley Dias was in 6th grade when she started collecting books.

BLACK GIRL BOOKS

Dias used social media to spread her idea. She started the hashtag #1000BlackGirlBooks. She quickly reached her goal. The **movement** spread. Dias collected 11,000 books.

Dias set out to make a change. She wanted to help other kids read more. She continues to help others.

Dias wanted to donate books to young girls in Jamaica because that is where her mother grew up.

CHAPTER 2

BACKGROUND

Dias was born on January 3, 2005.

She lives with her parents in New Jersey.

Her mom grew up in Jamaica. Her dad

was born in the United States.

Dias' mom runs an organization.
It is called GrassROOTS Community
Foundation. It helps people who are poor.
It helps women and children take care of
their health. Dias' parents love helping
people. Their kindness makes Dias want
to help people too.

Dias was born in
New Jersey.

Dias went to Ghana, Africa, in 2015. She worked with African Health Now. They had a health fair. Dias helped people take care of their teeth. She also tested people's blood pressure.

Many children in Ghana are very poor.

TIES TO AFRICA

Dias has relatives from islands near Africa. She feels connected to Africa. She wants to help people who live there.

CHAPTER 3

HELPING
Others

Dias wanted to continue to help others. She started with people in her community. Dias got together with more than 20 girls. They started the SuperGirls Society.

The group helped homeless teens.

Sometimes homeless teens stay in **shelters**.

The SuperGirls made the teens' rooms better.

They added books and decorations. They also

bought health and beauty items for the teens.

Dias has a passion for helping others.

Dias said that her mom (right) inspires her to help others.

Dias is always looking to help others. She wants to make the world a better place.

A GROWING LIBRARY

Dias and others gave books to a library in New Jersey. This library now has thousands of books about black girls.

CHAPTER 4

MEDIA
Promotion

Dias wanted to tell her ideas to the world. In 2016 she became a guest **editor**. She worked with *Elle* magazine. She wrote articles online.

Dias started her own zine for *Elle*. It is called *Marley Mag*. A zine is an online magazine. The articles are about change. One guest post said books should show more **Muslim** characters.

Dias once spoke at the White House at an event for *Elle* magazine.

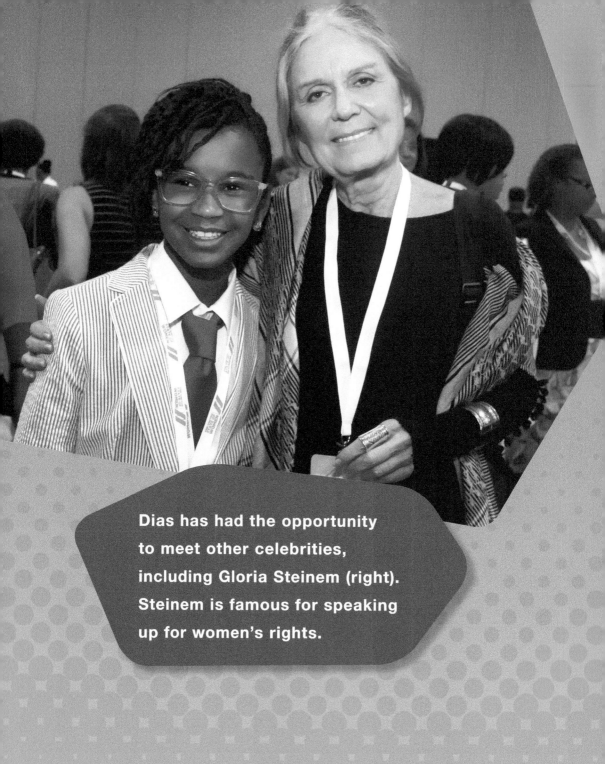

Dias has had the opportunity to meet other celebrities, including Gloria Steinem (right). Steinem is famous for speaking up for women's rights.

MORE OPPORTUNITIES

Dias also interviewed people for *Marley Mag*. She spoke with Hillary Clinton in 2016. Clinton was running for president. Dias asked Clinton about books and friends. She also asked Clinton about middle school.

Dias later went on television. She told people about her movement. She went on Ellen DeGeneres' talk show in 2016. Dias spoke about her goals. DeGeneres gave her $10,000 for her project.

Dias won a Distinguished Service award at the 5th Annual Foundation for Letters Gala in 2016.

CHAPTER 5

AUTHOR

Dias wrote a book in 2018. It is called *Marley Dias Gets It Done: And So Can You!* The book is about **activism**. It is about getting people involved in the community.

Dias believes **charity** is not activism.

She thinks charity is a good thing.

But activism means more. It means

taking action.

Dias believes it's important to educate yourself and follow your passion.

Dias' book guides people. It tells them how to become involved in their communities. Dias tells people to choose a problem. She tells people how to make a plan. Then they will make a difference.

Dias enjoys speaking to others about activism.

Dias wants to continue to make a difference.

Dias is young. But this doesn't stop her. She continues to help others. She wants to change the world.

GLOSSARY

activism
the use of action to go against or support a cause

character
a person or animal in a fiction story

charity
something given to help people in need

editor
a person who writes and edits for a magazine

inspired
to be filled with an emotion or idea

movement
an organized effort by people with a common goal

Muslim
a believer in the religion of Islam

shelter
a place for people to stay when they do not have homes

TIMELINE

2005: Marley Dias is born.

2015: Dias starts her book drive movement #1000BlackGirlBooks.

2016: Dias interviews Hillary Clinton.

2016: Dias appears on the *Ellen* show.

2017: Dias donates 11,000 books.

2018: Dias' book is published.

ACTIVITY

CREATE YOUR OWN GRASSROOTS ACTION PLAN!

Write your own plan for a grassroots organization. Name a problem in your neighborhood, country, or world. Next, think of one or two ways to help solve this problem. Last, write your grassroots action plan. Use the following steps to guide you in your writing:

- How will you get people to join your organization? Write a one to two paragraph plan.

- What steps will you take to make the change? Write a list of the steps.

- How will you keep track of your goals and if they are met? Create some way to track your goals. This could be a list, spreadsheet, or Word document.

- Sum it up! Write a summary of your grassroots organization. It should describe who you are and what you do.

FURTHER RESOURCES

Want to read as much as Marley Dias? Check out these websites with book lists:

Children's Books Council Lists:
http://www.cbcbooks.org/reading-lists

GrassROOTS Foundation Black Girl Books Database:
https://grassrootscommunityfoundation.org/1000-black-girl-books-resource-
    guide

Want to learn more about Dias and her favorite books? Read these books:

Dias, Marley, with Siobhan McGowan. *Marley Dias Gets It Done: And So Can You!*
    New York: Scholastic Press, 2018.

Woodson, Jacqueline. *Brown Girl Dreaming*. New York: Nancy Paulsen Books,
    2014.

INDEX